The

MW00880803

Instruction Manuel for
Intentional Misleading Fabrication

by James O'Reilly

How to use this book as a reference:

The Keyword Chapter has page numbers of those keywords so that you may directly go to the section for that pretext. If you are using the Kindle edition the keywords will be linked to the specific location by page number. The page numbers for each keyword may slightly differ between print and ebook editions.

James has put together a thorough compilation of pretext scripts and methods in which to implement them. With perfect instruction, James makes explaining the pretext processes make sense the first time you read it. This is exactly what investigators need. Loaded with advice for investigative newcomers.
--Mark Wall, L. A. Investigations

Undoubtedly, this book is an excellent reference to make one a master of the art of surveillance.
--Tina Sewell, Gray Hawk Agency Dublin

Overall good investment for the professional. James O'Reilly presents all-inclusive accounts of an experienced detective.
--Laurie Sanchez, Blue Moon L.A.

A personal note from James:

Many of these pretexts have been passed around from one working private eye to another and there are many of them that I used as a detective in law enforcement. Do you have a question? Do you need some help with a sneaky pretext that you're working on? Just drop me a note in email and I'll be glad to help you out.

100% of the profit of this book is going to my daughter's law degree. If you enjoy it and find it an asset to your investigation tool box please let other investigators know about it so that they can have it in their tool box and my daughter can be a *great lawyer*.

Follow me on Twitter @itsJamesO

Connect with me on LinkedIn
James@hiredgunpub.com

What exactly is pretexting anyway?

A pretext is a carefully manipulated act to gain factual evidence that you would not otherwise be able to naturally discover. Some investigative folks call it a gag or a scam. But, for the purpose of staying on track in this book, I will always call it a pretext. The purpose of this book is to bring a wide variety of pretext ideas that work in today's working class age of internet and smart phones with overall scam awareness in the general public.

A major part of skip tracing includes some type of pretext styled to fit the target's circumstances. We just simply can't do now, in detective work, what we could do 20 or even 10 years ago on an investigation. But, there are more things that we can do than ever before. Although some good ole' standards remain, we have to be resourceful and wise regarding the law.

Table of Contents

An Irish Blessing

May the road rise to meet you,
May the wind be always at your back,
May the sun shine warm upon your face,
May the rains fall soft upon your fields,
And, until we meet again,
May God hold you in the hollow of His hand

Introduction

I promise I won't hurt your eyes and waste brain power by giving you my history in law enforcement, investigations and skip tracing. Just know that I have been doing it since I got out of high school and I am over sixty years old. You can ascertain my ability by the subject matter covered in this book. I am not one for blabbering, and verbose instruction won't be found in these pages. I will not quote law. I will provide links to them, and I may summarize laws that are particularly important to pretexting.

The only forewarning you will get is that not all circumstances for pretexting are legal. If you're in collections, you already know you're not allowed to use any type of pretext whatsoever. If you're a debt collection skip tracer you're not allowed to skip trace to find lost loves, parties to adoption or any skip tracing that is not collections related. Any other type of skip tracing can only be done by a licensed private investigator, law enforcement, process servers and bail enforcement officers. If you do illegal skip tracing, you may find yourself losing your business, in jail and possibly be the defendant in a *very* expensive lawsuit.

If you're working in collections, you will know as you're being trained what laws are meant for you. The same goes with bounty hunting, serving papers and investigations. If you're a paralegal or an attorney, you'll also know that you can subpoena account information as soon as you discover it exists. The same is nearly true for judgment collections. You should know what your boundaries are. Sometimes the simplest of processes can backfire and create a mess that you'll have to go back to clean up.

The first rule in pretexting is to protect your identity. Think through every minute detail of your pretext through the eyes of the target and make sure that you experience the pretext in your mind (not just imagining your desired results) with reason. Using a practical "think it through" method, you can judge if your pretext idea will be rational, realistic and get the information that you're targeting.

After working in investigations for a while you will realize that you have been catapulted into people's personal lives and will have experiences that give you a third eye and sixth sense about approach.

Every pretext ever contrived was based on need or greed. The golden rule is everybody wants something for nothing. If you pretend to give a little something away, you might get pay dirt in return. The fundamental necessities in life are water, food, shelter and love. The core method of pretexting takes those basic needs and creates an opportunity to use greed (coupled with a little need) as encouragement for the target to take the pretext bait.

As your investigation unfolds and you examine the lifestyle of your target, it could be pretty easy to decide what kind of pretext that you want to do. The more you know about the target of a pretext, the better you can get them to believe what you present. A good investigation will uncover opportunity and help you put a personalized plan into action.

I have never done a pretext on a minor. Not in law enforcement or in my career thereafter. I don't think that there's ever a good pretext to use on someone underage. Most minors don't have checking accounts, bank loans or assets of any kind. I haven't ever seen a minor child be a subject to a lawsuit. I stand firm on the ethic that I will not do a pretext with the target being a minor (with the minor the actual target of a pretext) to get information on an adult. In a very rare blue moon, a child will answer the phone on a pretext phone call. I have asked where someone is by name, and the child innocently answered in great detail.

Pretext Tool Box

Experience will teach you that revealing how you came across the information you're seeking could jeopardize your career with the exception of perhaps using a pretext for bounty hunting. An attorney won't be able to tell details about a pretext to a jury. Instead, the information that you reveal will be subpoenaed directly from the source.

Additionally, I don't have to tell you when you do your investigation if you discover the target has put furniture up for sale on Craig's List or may have a "free puppies" sign in the front yard, to just go with the flow. Just call them up and be someone who needs a new puppy or a used couch.

For instance, if you do a pretext to discover what insurance company someone has for homeowner's insurance. The attorney would directly subpoena the insurance company for policy owner information and not reveal how the information came to them.

Regardless, there are many databases that provide information to get you close to your target. You're just taking it a step beyond to get what you can't find in a public database, or a non-public professional database and get verification beyond the shadow of a doubt.

When taking ideas and acting out scenarios in this book, realism is utterly and extremely important. If you're putting out cards for a free grass cutting, hang them on the target's neighbor's doors as well. When you pull up to meet the property owner that you're targeting, have your lawn mower in the back of your truck. Shake their hand, get your papers served and take off. If you're playing the role of a painter, then wear painted clothes. If you're a bum, make sure your big toe sticks out of your shoe.

I once had a Hooters restaurant open close to the office and Hooters girls came in bringing free hot wings to everyone in the building. And, yes, they wore their little Hooters outfits. What if those

Hooter's girls we on a fact finding mission? I'd say they could get anything they wanted from me! Who could resist a cute girl with free hot wings?

I have several vehicles reserved for surveillance and have magnetic door signs for most of the pretexts for realism. I get these on-line, and some sign companies can do them on same-day service. The ones that look the absolute best have the background color of the vehicle as the background of the sign. My white pick-up truck has magnetic signs for an electrician, with a red oval and a yellow lightning bolt through it. The white background blends into the door and from a distance, it's not easy to tell it's a magnetic door sign.

My wife helps me with pretexts as well. Women can get away with a lot more than a man. A sweet talking lady can schmooze her way to getting some maid service sold and a sweet little check from your target all the while getting to see the garbage first hand. My wife's been a maid, a party girl, a bag lady, and acted in countless of other roles. She is damn good at dressing the part for the role. If she's a down on her luck girl with a broke down car, I promise you'll never second-guess her.

Business cards, post cards other elements that get the pretext rolling for you all can be done in small amounts with on-line printing companies such as Vista Print. I keep my eye out for any freebies that I could use. Many of the promo items that they have could help you achieve realism in your pretext. Jim (Rockford Files) always typed his own fake business cards. Here you can order them in bulk.

I do pretext printing at home with my ink-jet printer. I buy 110 LB high gloss paper (I get this from a local printing company). It's heavy and shiny. This card stock makes a really nice post card that sticks out in the mail. I use these for mailers where I direct the target to go to a website and complete an entry form to win one room of furniture from a furniture store "opening" in the target's neighborhood. Keeping a selection of different types of card stock to print on is good. Invest in anything on sale and all the colors of the rainbow. I like blue and pink for mailing "advertising" from attorneys and orange and yellow for legal type notices.

Other basic tools that you'll need are disposable phone numbers and a way to put them out on the internet as a business listing. You probably already know about burner phones. Any prepaid cell phone that doesn't require your personal identification to register. Just remember that burner phones are for working and not pleasure. Never feel safe to make a personal phone call on your burner phone. That way there won't be a phone number dialed that can be connected directly to you or anyone in your team. Also, NEVER pay for your burner phone with anything but cash. Don't buy prepaid re-load cards with your credit card and never "top off" your burner phone minutes with personal credit card.

The trap line is the single most important investigative tool in any pretext. It has many times helped me do in just a few weeks what the FBI and California State Police couldn't do in ten years. When you use pretexting you will undoubtedly flush out the target and get a phone call on your trap line. Sometimes from a place of employment or a paramour's cell phone. Either or, you will get information that will get you results.

Google Voice is a free product that provides phone numbers free (U.S. only). You can have one phone number per email address, and the features are nice. It has texting and call blocking along with customizing the greeting. You can have someone say their name before the call is connected to you. I don't use that particular feature. I have all my Google Voice accounts set up so that no one can tell it's a Google Voice account.

It's been pretty clear in the success of using local numbers for trap lines versus toll-free numbers that people will trust a local phone number over a toll-free number (since that collection calls are known to use toll-free phone numbers). I get a near 100% good response from using a Google Voice number forwarded to a cell phone that has a Trapcall subscription on it.

I can also make outgoing calls from a Google Voice account. This puts my Google Voice phone number on caller ID to whomever I am calling. It's the same process as spoof calling except your phone number isn't a fake. In addition, with texting, if I have the texting feature turned on in Google Voice and forwarded to my burner phone, when I return a text, it will have my Google Voice phone number and not my cell phone number. Remember Batman, protecting your real identity is top priority.

Other great things to use with a cell phone in pretexts are Trapcall.com and Spooftel.com. Using Spooftel will give the target reassurance as most people have confidence in their caller ID display. When you call from Pizza Hut to offer a free medium two topping pizza in exchange for an email address to send coupons, you will want to use a local store's phone number.

They may even have your pretext number programmed into their cell phone already as "Pizza". Gaining trust of the target leaves you with an opening to get more information. You may need to know if there are kids in the house, or simply need a psychical address for the target.

Getting your pretext phone number into a Google, Bing and Yahoo search results is quite easy when using Manta and Merchant Circle. Both free sites allow you to create a listing with or without the pretend business address made public. Another way to get your phone number into a search engine is to list it in 800notes.com, mrnumber.com or tnid.us with notes as if you're someone who received a phone solicitation from that phone number.

Looking at other listings, there are dates posted on all entries. I suggest making a mild tempered comment such as, "This is a local lawn company asking if I need my grass cut or trees trimmed." Vista Print also has a directory listing for $2.50 a month. This is the only cheap website hosting that I have seen contents appear in a Google search just a few days later.

Making your pretext search engine optimized in this internet age is a pretty important aspect of realism. Some sites such as complaintsboard.com and ripoffreport.com will give your pretext company some age and depth as a real company. With a few mild and "resolved" complaints that can be found by a target while researching your pretext company, you can give your target assurance that your company is real. Not to mention, these complaints pop up in search engines nearly from the first day that they go live.

Gated communities with live guards can be somewhat difficult to overcome. Live guards are supposed to let you in so that you can serve papers. The downfall is some communities won't allow you to go into the neighborhood by yourself and a security officer tagging along or parked behind your car is a red flag that won't get the door answered. A service-based pretext could get you past the gate without the escort, and you would need to use the phone or mail to get your bait advertising to your target.

A few standard props such as a lighted pizza chain sign that attaches to the roof of a car, and some pizza delivery uniforms could come in really handy (all restaurant props can be found at restaurant supply stores). One of Los Angles' bigger gate communities requires the driver show a delivery receipt with the address the driver is delivering to. It's possible that the local pizza delivery restaurant is on the list to allow entry so that the homeowner doesn't have to remember to call the gate to inform the guard every time pizza is ordered.

If you get creative with a pretext and require information to be input by a keypad on a phone, the recording of entered digits can and be played into a pager service, and the recorded digit's input will appear on the pager screen. I haven't used this in many years however; this may also work with a cell phone paging option.

Apartment complexes with gates that require a card to get in or out, most repo men that I know get these cards from repos out of apartment complexes. I have had stacks of these cards and just take a marker and write the address and apartment name on each one. Everyone once in a while one key card will work for a different apartment complex. I just park my car and walk over the unit trying every card in my stack. People that come by just think I am working on the unit.

Newer technology has given us one handy little device that blocks cell phone signals. I have one covertly wired into my dashboard in my car. It's a unit that churches and schools are allowed to use but the actual box is not legal. There are websites that will sell these devices to you and ship from China. Just send them an email and tell them you are a private school or a church. I have a unit that will stop a signal for 600 feet around my car. It's wired into the car and has a toggle switch to turn it on.

Cyber Tracking

Enticing someone to go to a website can sometimes seem like a long shot. Especially if you're using a sweepstakes entry form pretext. You might try to use a simple pre-approved credit card pretext but don't ever ask for a social security number or date of birth. Some web hosting sites don't allow this type of form asking for that information at all and your site will be taken down.

The only one that I have seen that will allow this type of personal information request is Godaddy.com, which is safer. You can buy the secure web server package for a flat yearly fee which encrypts the forms submitted. Just don't allow Godaddy to display the Godaddy secure badge on your site. You can remove it yourself, just ask customer service how and they will direct you. I think the little Godaddy.com logo would be a deterrent on a good on-line pretext. How many finance companies do you know that use Godaddy?

Godaddy has the nicest customizable form template on their basic hosting plan. You can do one simple page or several. I personally choose to do one page. Always pattern your site after studying another one similar to your idea. If your idea has a match that uses one page, go with the single-page format. Keeping it simple is a huge plus on a pretext such as a sweepstakes entry or an on-line credit application.

If you're looking for personalization on this type of pretext simply use a reference number on the offer letter and request that number on the application. I send out hundreds of this type of pretext in a month, and I keep track of the reference or "invitation" numbers on a spreadsheet along with the name and address I mailed to. If I get mail returned to me, I just go to the name and highlight the address in red, so I know it's a dead (no good) address.

A newer form of advertising comes in texting (text blasting) to cell phones. It's often that I have a cell phone number to bust and can't because it's a burner phone. There is no database that can bust this phone number with, maybe it's too new or the target hasn't applied for credit using the number. I really haven't anything else to go on but some creative texting. I use a combination of several different web services to pull this type of pretext off.

Getting the texting service setup is affordable and easy to do. I use dialmycalls.com and there are a few other text "blasting" services out there similar to it. With the texting service, you can buy a keyword such as PIZZAHUT or COUPON paired with a five-digit number. You have to verify a phone number with the service, and I use a Google Voice phone number for these types of purchases.

I also use a pre-paid Visa gift card for these on-line purchases (Remember Batman, protect your identity). After you get all set up you can send a text to your own burner phone to test it out. You can see that your text will look something like this:

(COUPON) Get a free entree register at getafreedinner.com

There won't be a phone number, only the text with the keyword and the five-digit pin number. When I registered my account, I used a phone number that has been long disconnected. I don't want call backs for these types of pretexts and there is a selection for getting a text back. If you should choose to use it, it's there.

So, if you're using a website, you'll just have a form that can be filled out to get a free dinner coupon. If there is only one target, and you're not doing a mass text blast; there won't be any difficulty in determining who is completing the online form. If you're looking to trap an IP address, there will be no question as to what case it's related to.

As far as I can tell thus far in my experience, Godaddy doesn't trap IP addresses. For this important feature, I use webs.com, which also has a free service. I use the subscription-based service so that the "Build a free website at webs.com" won't be at the footer of the page. To get the IP trapping turned on you will have to go to the Website Statistics selection on the Control Panel and activate the free Clicky service. Clicky is great. It will give you the IP address, tell you how the target is connecting to the site (cell phone and screen size), tell you how long they were on and what web server used.

If you're gathering this information in preparation of a subpoena, you will know what provider to send that subpoena to and what IP address is being connected to that internet service provider. The prize will be the address and the name the service is in.

Using UPS

I send mail to targets all the time. For many different pretexts and the first thing I need to figure out is if the target even lives there. Sending a post card with dismissive unimportant advertising on it could be returned letting you know that your target doesn't live there, or if the residence is vacant. The best possible result is that my mail is forwarded, and I get back a forwarding address in the mail.

Uniformly printed and discretely, "Address Service Requested" is under my return address, incidentally that return address is always a retail mail box rental. If there is any mail forwarding on file, I get back a bigger post card and have to pay fifty cents for this forwarding address service.

Cautious people don't really accept certified letters anymore. Especially if they know they have debt and a lawsuit may ensue. When I have papers to serve in my county to a defendant who is out of town, I can send those papers via certified mail. The service is only good if it's registered mail and signed for by the defendant. One maneuver that has worked for me in the recent past is sending the papers in a box and sending the box registered and certified mail or FedEx where a signature is required by the recipient. Who wouldn't want to see what is in a big box?

A private case I worked on just a few years ago was made successful with using a mailer from New York City. My wife sat down and created a mail piece from a major network television station inviting the target to audition for a reality show that was explained with a dating theme. The target was "nominated" in an online form and the target was required to call for background screening before the audition details were given. Hook, line and sinker. We nabbed our guy.

An older pretext that most experienced investigators are familiar with is the door hanger or post card that says, "We have a delivery for you." And, "Sorry we missed you! Please call us at 1-800-get-mail to reschedule delivery." Of course, you're using either your burner phone number with Trapcall.com or using a toll-free trap line. I have seen other investigators use a door hanger that looks exactly like the yellow and brown UPS notice. It's a large pre-printed sticky note giving a trap line number for delivery to be rescheduled. UPS uniforms are hard to get on line. I think UPS has a dedicated person that buys up all the UPS uniforms that get put up for sale on the internet as I have never been able to find any.

When using a delivery pretext, most people buy things on the intent now. Amazon is a big competitor for Walmart.com and one gives free shipping, 99 cent shipping and so on and so on. If you pretext a person that you are working for a major delivery company and that you have a damaged package that you think belongs to their address, it was damaged in the most recent natural disaster (Hurricane, earthquake) and the address label is illegible and the inserted packing slip is also damaged.

"Can't tell you what is in the box but can give you a value of $300.00 is what it's insured for. Where do I deliver it? And someone has to be there to sign for it. Company regulates don't allow us to leave it at the door. " Another angle would be a FedEx from the hospital records office of a hospital known to the target.

Mail fraud is not mail fraud unless your pretext is fishing for credit information, or you're asking for money. Since you won't ask for money, there shouldn't be any pretext where mail fraud would be committed. When you're engineering your pretext stay clear from anything that requires a target to give their social security number or date of birth.

You most likely already have this information anyway. Dealing with family members that share a name and have Jr. and Sr. on the end of their name, specifically ask for any name extensions that can help you determine if you're dealing with an older or younger generation. And of course, you will know instantly when you get your target on the phone if you're speaking to a Jr. or the senior.

If you decide to send out more than one type of mailer to a target make sure that no two mailers look alike or get mailed from the same zip code. When the stamp is cancelled-a machine will imprint the zip code of the processing center on the mail piece. If you have contacts (or friends) out of town, you can mail your pretext pieces to them, and you may also mail your mail pieces to the post office from which you want the mail to be sent from. Just address it to the post master at that station asking for the mail to be sent from there.

Don't cross your mailers. Use the same type of addressing (by hand, label & font on the label, or printed directly onto the mailer using a computer) on each pretext. Be real. If you send out a postcard to a target using a purple ink pen, then send out another entirely different pretext, using the same purple ink pen your target is going to throw your mailer in the garbage and be suspicious of future attempts to run a pretext.

Emotional manipulation may be inflicted by the type of mail a target receives. A damn difficult auto repossession once had me in fits. The car was a Lexus that had been on a high profile television show that does custom modifications then surprises the owner. The real story is that this Lexus was a lease, and the contract was over. The car had been sequestrated, and the owner was nowhere to be found. In one day, I printed over ten letters from different attorneys offering criminal-defense services on the recent "criminal action" filed against the target. I mailed them from different zip codes all around the city of Los Angeles. In less than 48 hours I received a phone call with an address where the car could be picked up.

One of the biggest and most successful mass pretext ever used in law enforcement was for a warrant round up. Mail sent out to people with open warrants from a local Los Angeles radio station gave a phone number to call for free concert tickets to the hottest gig in town. The Eagles and even Flock of Seagulls were part of the pretext. Of course, there was no free concert and when people walked into the stadium they were directed to a line where their ID was check.

People were either handcuffed or sent to another area of the stadium where they would have to wait until the "free concert" was over and leave freely as to not disturb the traffic that continued to enter the arena.

On-line resources for mail box centers out of state that can handle your outgoing mail are really nice to use. I always include a test piece of mail that would go to one of my own post office boxes locally. Just to make sure they are sent. I can say there was a time I sent mail out with first class postage already affixed to the mailers, and the entire package went missing.

Just so you know when dealing with an out-of-town company you may want to put in some safe guards such as a smaller count of mailings. These types of advertising postcards and letters that I send from out of town usually are just enticements to get someone to go on line to my trap website, so I don't use "Address Service Requested" and sometimes I don't even use the targets name. I use "To Our Favorite Customer or Targets Name" so that the mail is delivered to anyone who lives in the house.

Social Strategy

So, you got lucky and found your target on social media or a dating site. I'm pretty sure I don't need to tell you what to do, but I'll tell you to stick to the first rule of pretexting: protect your identity. Flirting on-line could be flirting with disaster. Keep it simple, don't ask too many leading questions in the beginning and make sure your pictures are irresistible and compatible with the target that you're pursuing. That rule remains true for Facebook, LinkedIn or any other site where you're connecting to your target person-to-person.

Tip: Are you being ignored? How pushy should you be? Just drop what you are doing that isn't working and start fresh with something else.

I have read lots of good information and put it to the test regarding tricks used on Facebook. This is the number-one way to find family and friends of anyone that you're looking for. Privacy is not important and connecting with family and friends is what social media is all about. Before we had Facebook and MyLife.com I used Ancestry.com which is not at all perfect and can get costly. Blending your search strategy with other free on-line sites can bring your investigation to a satisfying level.

In the Recommended Reading chapter, there is a book called Skip Trace Secrets that plainly lays out how to use Facebook's hacks and other on-line social gathering sites to your advantage. The author has a blog listed in the book where she, and other investigators and skip tracer's, post articles about skip tracing. If you're new to the investigative world or want to get to the heart of locating people with the new technology that's out there, Skip Trace Secrets is an excellent book to keep as a reference on your desk (I have mine on my cell phone).

Auto Pretexts

The bulk of civil suits that I serve subpoenas for are auto accidents where the 'at fault' party is either uninsured or under insured. Witnesses and litigants can be difficult to serve if you can't find them. There is only so much information on a police report. If the officer didn't get phone numbers and ask for current addresses the only information could be an outdated drivers license address. The other small sector of auto-related papers that I serve are for final balance judgments and sequestration orders. With a sequestration order, I can block a car in and have it impounded. I don't have to serve the defendant as long as the court order is signed by a judge.

If I know what someone is driving, or I have a sequestration order for an auto; one pretext that I have used in the past is to make contact with anyone close to the target. If I can't get to the target directly, and tell them that I am an accident investigator and their car has been involved in a hit-and-run accident. I explain that I must see the car to verify that there is or is not consistent damage with the police report. Hit and run charges in most states are felonies, and I continue to ask many questions about who has been driving the car and exactly where the car has been driven.

The target will want to deny involvement but be firm and demand to see the auto, as hiding the car could mean criminal charges for the target, especially if the "hit and run" accident has caused a personal injury and extensive property damage.

Most cities have red light cameras in major intersections to pump up revenue. A mail pretext would be to contact the target with a bill for running a red light that was caught on camera. Most big cities use an outside collection agency to collect this type of ticket related fine revenue and because no one signs for the ticket, and it's caught on camera.

The only threat that the city or county government can do is intervene with the state registration, or threaten to revoke the license until the ticket is paid. Of course, the phone pretext would be to collect the red light camera ticket fine, just make sure you use the required by law mini-Miranda when making a phone call (even if it's a pretext) to collect a debt. Keep it real, keep it unemotional and simple.

One of the more difficult things to find out in a database is who the target's insurance provider would be. I have tossed it up between offering a huge discount for switching with verification of current insurance. Heck, the policy number and insurance company information will do. Remember everyone wants something for nothing. Offering free road side assistance along with free rental-car reimbursement for an "at fault" accident could make someone take the time to listen to you and give you the information that you're after.

When a car is purchased from a dealership regardless if it's a cash purchase or financed, proof of insurance must be provided for the title transfer. Other instances where auto insurance is required to be shown would be to renew state registration and possibly state inspection. If a dealer is carrying the note on an auto, there may be good insurance in the file. It could take a subpoena to get that information, but I have pretexted buy-here-pay-here dealers as another car lot looking for the same debtor.

I ask for insurance info with the explanation that there may be an additional driver on the policy that could help you find your repo. Make sure to let the car dealer know that you will share any new information if their cars should happen to go out for repossession too.

Since insurance can be used as a second ID in some circumstances such as renting a USPS post office box, and it happens to be the law to carry insurance in all fifty states looking into these angles with pretexts can be ideal. When insurance is sold the underwriter may pull a credit report and be listed in the inquiry section and all insurance companies report policy information to the state where the coverage is purchased. If you know a police officer that can run a license plate, insurance information may come up on the vehicle information.

Phone Pretexts

Phone investigations can be the golden ticket if no database gives you results. With the popular and widespread use of cell phones, investigations can get expensive. Paying for cell phone busts on each and every cell phone number listed in phone records can lead to nowhere. Pretexting directly to the target can save a small bundle and keep you from breaking any other laws such as pretexting the phone company for detail call records. And, thanks to George Bush Jr. this is now a federal offense.

Another profoundly illegal pretext is any call to a financial institution such as a credit union or a bank. I have read some opinions on the law (GLB) that say it's illegal to pretext ANYONE to get banking information. That means if you pretext a business asking for the target's banking information, and get caught, you may suffer some consequences. There are plenty of other things to try instead. Road bumps may come out of nowhere, but it's better to be safe than sorry.

Calling the target asking for a wrong name, using the same name with a different last name or a similar name just to determine if someone is home or who is home. I once had my grandson call a target from a burner phone asking for his mother. "Mom?", (he is such a good little actor) "I need Mom, where's Mom?" The person on the phone said that he had a wrong number and there are no ladies in the house. This is exactly what I needed to know since my target was a woman on the run.

If you need to smoothly get out of a phone call, I suggest saying something like, "Hello? Hello? Are you there? I can't hear you, your cutting in and out…" After a few seconds just end the call. Collection agencies ask for the first name of the person that answers the phone if the target says they have a wrong number. The excuse is that the debt collector needs to put a note on the account letting future collectors know that the person they are attempting to collect from has changed their phone number and not to call this "wrong number" again.

High school reunion, calling to get mailing address for reunion party venue and RSVP invitations. This is great if you already know what high school the target when to. There are a few people that like to make the reunions and want to know about get-togethers.

The local chain pharmacy letting you know that your Vicodin prescription is ready. Yes, tried and true, this works. Who wouldn't want their Vicodin?

New mom with baby: coupon for 10.00 or gift certificate for registering on a toy store or children's clothing website. Major store chains that have a gift certificate and points program and DSL Shoes, Pet Smart, Olive Garden Restaurant has a gift certificate for doing a survey. Large chains that people get rewards from that can be used in pretexting: Best buy, Office Depot, Office Max, Radio Shack, Pet Smart. And, of course, they want your email so that they can email you the stores sales paper and sales events for preferred customers.

Flower store making delivery and the driver can't find your address, driver out in the car with flowers. This is especially good if there has been a death in the family and the funeral is over. Pretexting the funeral home is another angle. But birthdays, Valentine's day and Mother's Day are other flower sending dates that could be good for this pretext.

Hospital survey: local big hospital, were admitted into the ER recently. Would like to ask some questions about the nursing staff that assisted you in the ER. It's highly practiced for a hospital staff to contact a patient after being released. Be prepared to hear any complaints and be genuine regarding righting any wrongs.

Tip: When calling a utility service or customer service to pretext, if you get a uncooperative rep on the line, hang up and call again to get a different person.

Big name restaurants do what is called a "mock service" before they open a new restaurant. This is so the staff and kitchen can prepare the menu, staff and bar can get on the job training and make sure the operation runs smoothly. Invitations to a mock service usually look like wedding invitations that include an RSVP form. A great pretext to use is to call the target and explain that there are seven new entrées on the menu and there will be a mock service by invitation only. Tell the target their name was on a list of people to call that are friends and associates of owners and servers at the restaurant. Where do they want the door tickets mailed to?

You have the name of an associate of the target, call target or visa versa, telling them they were listed as a reference on a jail bond and that person missed a court date. Ask for contact information and give trap line or call from trap line on caller ID.

Late notice for utility: can go many ways, calling to notify of a shut off date, opens a line of communication regarding last payment made and how it was made. Verify connection address and name on utility with target. Calling the utility company as the target wanting to pay off an old bill is one angle, calling to get the account number to pay at a pay center (usually a grocery store) is yet another angle.

When pretexting the utility companies calling to ask what the service address they have it or the mailing address on file, tell them you need the account number to pay the bill at the local grocery store or put on your money order for the night drop. I always say I left the bill at work and time is of the essence. I always have all the information of the target and most likely the account can be pulled up by the phone number.

One suggestion is to pretext a utility saying that you (as the target) have inherited money from your grandfather and you want to pay off all your outstanding bills. Of course, you don't have an account number but you have your social security number. Or, you are calling to take care of the deceased persons account.

For a business- you're a reporter for a community newspaper or a city wide newspaper and you would like to highlight the target business for the paper. This leaves you wide open to ask business related questions that would apply to your investigation. I have a laminate that I hang around my neck that says MEDIA and gives my "name" and the name of the publication I am a reporter for.

Tip: When you hear loud children in the background don't let the target escape. Just say how cute the children sound.

Unlisted land line pretext, the 911 Office is calling because the address provided to the office is incomplete. Need the address to be verified either on the phone or in person by the city fire station personnel. New neighborhoods that are developed turn in the maps to the 911 office, which in turn assigns an address to each house as it's built. If your Garmin or Tom Tom doesn't locate the address it's because it's too new and has not been updated into the maps from the county office. A flipside 911 pretext is calling the target spoofing 911 on the phone caller ID and saying that someone from that phone just called 911 and is everything alright? Get name and address information for the "records" and advise that police will respond to 911 calls and, "Please don't let the children play with the phone."

Have a phone number but need an address? Call the phone number and advise the person answering that I am from the local electric (or phone) company and I will be shutting down the power on their street for 5-6 hours. I think ask if there is anyone on life support at their residence or if it would be a major inconvenience... If they answer yes (and they do), I tell them that I would be able to leave their power on and to confirm their address, they will give their power won't be turned off.

You can also be a line repairman calling from the phone company and simply ask in a logical conversation "What block are you in?" Tell the target that you have the lines in front of you and the schematic is on the way for the lines. You don't want to send their home phone to someone else's house!

Calling the target as a triage nurse from a doctor's office to make sure the appointment time is confirmed and that the prescription has been called into the local pharmacy.

To get banking info, place of employment and current address: call from a local bank: "This is Citizens Bank and you have been pre-approved for a VISA card with 5% interest and no fees for the first year." If they say yes, then you can get address, current job and other phone numbers to confirm the application.

Call the target from their cell phone company and tell them that their phone number has been cloned to another phone. Ask if they have received any strange phone calls or texts. Ask if they would meet an area rep that would bring them a loaner phone as you need their phone to catch the crooks. Meet and swap phones. The phone you give will have spy ware on it to trap text messages and phone calls. Tell them you will give them free months service for their troubles and the new phone is on the house. You may also use FedEx (for realism) for some documents if you don't really want the actual cell phone.

You're calling from Macy's in central Chicago, and they were pre-approved for a $500.00 store credit card with a $50.00 gift certificate. Continue to obtain mailing address. Must sign for package due to theft as gift certificates are sent via FedEx.

Another way to get realism is to submit an application in the targets name so that the decline letter will go to the address they give you and they won't be calling you back saying, "Where's my card?"

A pre-surveillance pretext used prior to starting various cases where a time frame a can be established in order to save our client's budget. Usually a female op makes a call to our subject indicating she's conducting a survey on the radio listening habits of individuals in the "name of city" area. The key questions are: What radio stations do you listen to when you drive to and from work and what times of day. Have several different questions at hand that refer to what shows and disk jockeys the target listens to.

It's possible that an older person may get the local newspaper delivered to the door. If you have a phone number and need an address, you may be able to pretext the local newspaper delivery to get the delivery address by stating that you're the target and the newspaper has not been received for an entire week asking what address that the newspaper has on file. I end the call with demanding the delivery driver throw the paper closer to the house so that it doesn't get stolen.

Another way to get an address of a target is to call when the target isn't home, tell the person answering the phone that you sent a Christmas or birthday card to the target and it was "returned to sender". Ask for a new mailing address. You can be an old friend from high school, a church lady or old co-worker.

It wouldn't be the greatest idea ever to impersonate any federal or state agency but I know there are quite a few targets that have come across my desk that received some type of welfare benefits. As long as people think that they are getting free money you don't have to use any IRS or government agency in a pretext.

A harmless way to discover where a business banks is to call the accounting office and explain that your checks were stolen and one of the stolen checks was written to the business for a specific amount on a certain date. Did the merchant get any ID info for this check? What was the check for? What is the name of the branch manager where you deposited the check? You need this because you filed a police report and the office wants to speak to the bank where the check was deposited.

In reality, the bank's name usually is on the back of the check with the account number where deposited, you may explain that you ordered the check front and back for the police report. I get away with saying that the police officer instructed you to get this information. Playing the part of a dumb victim goes a long way.

To get the caller name and phone number of a cell phone, call the number and spoof the caller ID to look like an out of the country phone number. Your role is that of an international operator. Tell the person that answers the phone that an international phone call was placed and the target's phone number was given for billing the charges to. Ask the target if any phone call was placed to a phone number in New York City and if they knew anyone in New York. Ask the target if they received a phone call from another operator to approve those charges. Then ask for the callers billing name and address.

Confirm the phone company as Verizon, AT&T, as you should already know what phone company that the target has for a cell phone. Even if it's a burner phone, you can figure this out in many ways.

A simple pretext to a retail rental mail box in a bigger city where not everyone knows everyone would be calling the mail box rental place and telling the clerk that you closed your box and put in a mail forwarding over two weeks ago and you haven't gotten any mail. The clerk should confirm if there is mail in the box and maybe will tell you who the senders are.

I have had, many times in the past, a targets phone disconnected for non-payment. If I have no other way to make contact with the target, the phone carrier can be pretexted. Since all the pertinent information is already going to be at hand, this is usually a pretty easy and 100% successful pretext on the phone company. You are simply asking for the phone to be turned back on, and either putting minutes on the phone or asking for five to ten more days of phone service citing a family emergency has taken place.

The most common excuse that works every time is to tell the customer service that your wife, husband, son or mother is in the ICU and you need the phone to keep contact with family that is out of town. You can go a step further by explaining that the patient in ICU is not expected to live through the week and please keep your phone on. Verizon does it, Cricket has done it and AT & T will do it as well.

A tried and true pretext to getting an address when all you have is a name and maybe a city or town. Call the local water company right in the middle of lunch time and tell them you're mad because you have very low water pressure and you want someone out to fix it right now. Give them your subject's name and tell them the last two times they came out to fix a problem they went to the wrong house. What address do your records show?

The jury duty pretext may have seen its better day as there are notices on most county websites around the country warning of such a scam. But, from another angle you may be able to get somewhere with it. Explaining to the target that the court house sent jury forms and that the court never received the forms back and the target didn't show for jury duty. Ask what address the forms should be sent to. I believe that the citizens of a county receive jury duty mail at the address used when they registered to vote.

So if you haven't already checked voter's registration, do that first. If the voters registration card has been returned to the county the on-line database will indicate that this address is not current or that mail has been returned. If this is the case this pretext will do just fine.

A common election year cold call is asking if the target is registered to vote. And, if not where can I send the forms to vote, or I can take that application over the phone for your registration. Have the voting poll locations open so that you can tell your target where to go vote. Ask if there is anyone there over the age of 18 whom you can get the voters registration done for and get the card out as soon as possible.

To find out if the subject's home address is good, call being a salesman for home siding and tell them you are in the area and if they would sit through your sales pitch you will give them a $35.00 gift certificate to (the hottest restaurant in town). This get's you in the house and lays them open to answer any questions you have because they want that gift certificate.

Pretext to remove customer's phone number from marketing database: Call the target and say you're from a big company such as Best Buy and tell the target that you're calling to confirm that the target's phone number has been removed from the database. Continue with that you're complying with federal law regarding the 'do not call' list, but since this is a big company you want to advise that a phone call may occur within the next two weeks as the system scrubs out the "do-not-call" phone numbers. Ask for the address to send a confirmation letter and a $10.00 gift certificate as a thank you for being so understanding about the process and that Best Buy is trying to make it better for their customers.

To find out if there is a man in the house: Call the target and ask for the man of the house, tell whoever answers the phone that you're a college student at (use your local college) and for a class you must conduct a neighborhood crime watch survey. After whoever has answered a few questions, ask to speak to the man of the house again (if there is indeed a man of the house). Continue with your line of questioning regarding neighborhood crime and any or particular questions you need answers to regarding a specific house on the street you may be also targeting.

A cold call to the man of the house could be to promote a new razor by a name brand manufacturer. Need address to mail full size product, could be a razor, shaving cream or famous men's cologne.

Call a neighbor and tell them the target has put them down as a reference for either buying a car, a personal reference on a job application, and continue a normal line of questioning for such a reference. Do you know where they work? Have they ever committed a crime?

In Person Pretexts

Live and in person pretexts should be practical. Never go alone, be a team and if you have to go alone have a car camera or recording device on you. Wear the uniform, have goodies such as pen's for giveaways and business cards for realism.

Neighbor moved- target of this pretext is any neighbor that lives next door to a recently moved target of your investigation. Ask old neighbors if they know where the target moved to. You borrowed something that belongs to them, or they borrowed something that belongs to you.

Going door to door with some fliers and asking
people to register to vote or sign a neighborhood
petition to get rid of something unsightly, add
playground equipment to a park or just put in
sidewalks, can be a winning ticket. One seemingly
innocent questionnaire is to do a demographic survey
of political party and take a "poll" of who the target is
expecting to vote for, if they have used early voting
or are planning to turn out at the polls in person.

Another effective pretext is where you would tell
someone that there are papers to be served to them
and ask for an address to meet the target. It's not
lawful to tell someone they are getting served papers
when there are no papers to serve and to serve
someone papers pretending the papers are another
kind of paperwork. There may be a difference in
saying this to someone versus doing this to someone.
It's been my experience people will flatly evade
service all the way around but it may get your phone
call returned due to curiosity.

Handing someone a pizza box with court papers inside is not suppose to be good service, but if you have no other way to get it done, then I guess do what you have to do. Some judges will say, obviously, the target showed up for court and call an end to any process of service dispute presented by the method of service.

Tip: Some pretexts are better when a flier is placed on the door instead of using the mail.

Neighbor's car out for repo, have you seen it? - A pretty simple pretext if you need to see who is inside a home, especially in the evening. I have used this before to gain the trust of a target, knocking on different days to see if I can get my target to answer the door and get papers served.

Getting bank account information could be as simple as shopping at the business and paying with a check. The reverse of this pretext would be to mail a rebate or refund check to the target and examine the back to see if it was deposited or cashed. A target may toss or lose a $5.00 check; I suggest that you make the sum from $20.00 to $30.00. That is about a tank of gas and it would be more likely to get attention.

Check the mailbox. I have never in my life taken someone else's mail, but I've been known to tip the door open to see if the mail is stacked up or if there is any at all. Just be delivering a flier to the door when you do such a thing, you can also throw a flier inside the box quickly. If you get confronted just play dumb.

Surveillance pretext of a land surveyor. Dress the part, orange vest, hard hat and some work boots. Camera on tall tripod won't be questioned. Most tripods are bright yellow with reflective tape down each leg. I did mine with florescent spray paint and heavy duty reflective tape I got at the hardware store. You can stand out there for hours pretending to be working and waiting for something. I've seen surveyors leaning on their tripod just "waiting" who knows for what.

I use small camera's that have infrared nodes around the lens for shady and dark recording. The fall back to those is they glow red in the dark. The good old Super 8 video cameras have night vision but they aren't small and concealable. You can find a variety of cameras on eBay. I keep a key chain camera on my keys all the time, and they do great with alternate light sources such as the porch light, head lights from my car or a flashlight.

It looks just like an alarm box and the buttons on the alarm box turn the camera off, tell it to take a picture, and tell it to start recording. These don't last a long time and setting the date and time can be a little taxing. The upswing is the key chain camera's are about 5.00 each on eBay and will record with your own micro SD card. The quality is pretty good too.

County road quality, door to door interviews asking about pot holes that need to be reported or street lights that are out or defective. Ask for names and phone numbers for people with complaints. Other road construction questions could be ditch culverts that are stopped up, man holes that have risen above road level and cracks in the road surface.

A bond jumper pretext (not to catch a real bond jumper) is one where you would door knock a street or apartment section with some mug shots of a perp asking the target if the perp is someone known to them. You can say, "Are you sure this isn't someone that works with you? Where to do you work?" Ask more question about groups, hobbies, etc... Then the target should commence spilling their guts about everything you need to know.

Fake (blank standard forms from the court house) subpoenas can be great tools as long as you aren't presenting them to the actual person who you decide the subpoena is for. Having a few blank subpoena forms can be useful. Fill one out with a non-related random name and door knock your target address asking questions about the fake person on the subpoena. Since the law states it is a crime to prevent service of process by either knowingly with words or psychical action, you can get the target to tell all.

This is your chance to ask the real target what you need to know. You can about whey they work, who their spouse is, who else may be living in the house. The questioning should be in a general nonchalant manner as the two of you would be trying to figure out if they know the mystery person and an explanation as to why the mystery person is using the real targets address.

A little trick to find out what time someone leaves the house is to use an analog watch and place it in the tire path. If it's dinky enough, driving over the watch will break it and the hands will be set at the time the watch was broken, giving you the time when the target drove out of the driveway.

A utility company may not call a customer but I have seen bright red or orange card stock door hangers (you can buy the star punch to make a hole for a door hanger) that say please call this toll free number, your power, cable or phone is about to be turned off for non-payment. This is a good pretext for a toll free number.

Getting into a gated apartment complex to see if your target's car is parked might take a bit of time, if you can't follow someone in or there is a live guard on the complex go visit the leasing office. Get the grand tour, ask questions and be a genuine apartment shopper. Ask to see a specific area of the complex, don't be shy. If your target has kids then you will know to look at two and three bedroom apartments. I have been in a few complexes where the families with kids are in one area and the renters without children are on the other side of the complex.

Have you ever been confronted on surveillance? There are a couple of really good excuses you can use for being there. If someone just walks up to your car because you're parked in front of their house, a good reason is that your alternator is out and your battery ran down. Let it be known that help is on the way.

If you're approached by a police officer you can let them know that you're waiting for your engine to cool. Or you could be doing a traffic count for the neighborhood that you are in. Or you could be looking for your lost dog, you heard from another neighborhood that he is sniffing around that street.

Another reason to be in the neighborhood is house hunting and you could also be driving around looking for your lost dog. Long surveillance may prompt you to call ahead to notify the local police department so that if they are called by a concerned neighbor they will know not to send anyone.

Verifying subjects ID - witness location, "my wife had an accident a few days ago and the police report said there was a "target's name" who was a witness. Are you the one that witnessed the accident? Follow that with a few "are you sure?" "it was a red Toyota Camry my wife was driving... you don't remember anything like that?"

Breaking down in front of targets house, knock door ask target to call a cab for you. Give trap line number to person that answers the door. Have the receiving line either be a detailed answering machine message or live person posing as dispatch.

Lost dog, have you seen my dog? Lost dog with different angle, "Is this your dog?" Always have a cute puppy in tow with a *secure* collar and leash on. You don't want your dog getting jerked out of your grasp!

Summaries of Law

The criminal element has overtaken pretexting in order to scam good people out of money and information to use in identity theft. In response to the advances in telephonic technology and types of scams that have been victimizing consumers, the government created laws that make pretexting illegal where there is an intention to trick financial information used to steal money from the consumer.

Telephone Records and Privacy Act of 2006
Obtaining toll records is now a federal offense. It bans pretexting of telephone companies and their customers for confidential phone records. It requires prior authorization from the customer. This is meant to include the detailed call records on a cell phone or home phone bill (VoIP is included as well I would imagine even though the laws don't specify VoIP, which is suspected to be amended at a future date).

Truth in Caller ID Act

No one in the U.S. may use spoofing caller ID with the intent to cause harm or obtain anything of value. That means I can't alter my caller ID to show that someone's bank is calling them to get account passwords or account numbers from a consumer. It has been a common practice for debt collectors to use caller ID spoofing to get someone to answer the phone. I have even heard reports of debt collectors making the consumers own phone number appear on caller ID.

The GLB

This act prohibits anyone in the U.S. from pretexting to obtain personal non-public financial information from any source, including banks. Your investigation efforts in database searches for non-public information must be accompanied by a permissible purpose, such as debt collection for a collection effort, and identity verification for a job applicant background check.

A professional database may audit your searches to make sure that you have permissible purpose (no more looking up old pals and past loves!).

The Deceptive Trade Practices Act

This act prohibits any person in the U.S. from pretexting to obtain anything of value from someone. Such as selling a fake time share and getting the money leaving the target as a victim of fraud. Any scam that would cause someone to give money for fictitious goods or services.

The FDCPA

This law pertains to consumer collections. A quick rundown of what is not allowed in a consumer collection, so that you won't mistakenly use it in a collection pretext.

- Threaten to garnish wages where wage garnishment is not allowed.

- Call every day until the debt is paid.

- Contact neighbors with debt information. But, you <u>can</u> ask for location of the debtor.

- Threaten imprisonment or criminal punishment.

- Report a financed vehicle as stolen due to past due payments.

- Say that you are an attorney, when in fact you are not.

- Contact employer about the debt.

- Threaten lawsuit when no lawsuit is really going to be filed.

- The Mini-Miranda Warning must be given to debtor.

- Cannot speak to anyone other than debtor and spouse about the debt.

Expectation of Privacy

I once knew a process server that used an infrared building scanner to see if someone was standing behind the door he was knocking on. To some, because he was not actually peeping inside a window, wouldn't be invasion of privacy. But, he actually was committing a crime. When getting your pretext underway you should never feel confident enough to break the law.

Trespassing is trespassing. Don't go in garages, don't try to open doors, and don't do what a normal door to door sales man wouldn't do. Don't feel entitled to break the law just because you have papers to serve or you feel safe because there's no one around.

Some exceptions to the rule are if a person posts information on a public forum such as an open Facebook or Myspace page. When information is accessed without a password or without illegally hacking, then it's public information. Such as asking questions on a public forum, or publicly making information available such as a phone number on a sign that says, "Free Puppies!"

There will always be a way to infiltrate the target. You have need and greed to work with. Both of those are provocative angles that yield fantastic results with patience and perfection. I have always said I'm not a thief. If you're not going to give it to me then I don't want it.

Recommended Reading

If you're like me, you will read everything you can get your hands on. This is how you discover tools and put a new twist on an old pretext. Skip tracing in general is an important term to search for on the internet. I have read everything and have my own recommendations. Please trust me when I say if it's not on the list don't waste your money.

Look for your states investigators association and get all the certification classes offered through the association. If you're already a licensed private investigator, you know who they are, if you're not yet licensed, find them through your state licensing office.

The Complete Idiot's Guide to Investigations by Steven Kerry Brown

Practical Method's for Legal Investigations by Dean Beers

Skip Trace Secrets - Dirty little tricks skip tracers use… by Valerie McGilvrey

The Private Investigation Handbook by Chuck Chambers

Social Engineering: The Art of Human Hacking by Christopher Hadnagy

Background Check by Valerie McGilvrey

Lying by Sam Harris

100 Subject Lines that Get Your Email Opened by Bard Williams

Easy Lie Detection by Mark Menefee

The Newbie's Guide on How to Conquer SEO by Andrea Kalli

The Private Investigators Legal Pocket Guide by Ron Hankin

Links Index

To determine if you're calling a cell, VoIP or land line:

www.fonefinder.net

www.phonevalidator.com

www.spydialer.com

www.superpages.com

www.whitepages.com

www.mrnumber.com

www.tnid.us

Spoofing

www.telespoof.com

www.spooftel.com

www.spoofcard.com

www.phonegangster.com

www.covertcard.com

www.freecalleridspoofing.com

www.crazycall.net

www.guerrillamail.com

Pay Databases

(Requires professional license)

www.accurint.com

www.IRBSearch.com

www.masterfiles.com

www.ustracers.com

www.mircobilt.com

www.tracersinfo.com

www.tlo.com

www.skipsmasher.com

www.skipmax.com

www.knowx.com

Text Blasting

www.dialmycalls.com

www.connectleader.com

www.ringcentral.com

Trap Line Service

www.trapcall.com For cell phones only

www.uccweb.com

www.ureach.com

www.bellscamp.com (Skiptracy)

Freebie Stuff

www.spokeo.com

www.pipl.com

www.veromi.com

www.kgbpeople.com

www.crimetime.com

www.zabasearch.com

www.411.com

Mail Box Forwarding & Remailer Service

www.mailboxrental.com

www.maillinkplus.com

www.lasvegasmailforwarding.com

www.usabox.com

www.myrvmail.com

SEO Your Pretext

These websites will get your pretext business on the front page of any Google, Bing, or Yahoo search.

www.Manta.com

www.Merchantcircle.com

www.Vistaprint.com

www.Webs.com

www.Wix.com

www.800notes.com

www.ripoffreport.com

www.complaintsboard.com

Did you enjoy this book? Please let other readers know by following the link below, remember, 100% of this book's profits go directly to my daughter's law degree. I *really* want her to be a great lawyer.

http://www.amazon.com/review/B00BHRMQ3O

HIRED GUN PUB

Disclaimer

I am in no way affiliated with Batman or The Rockford Files. This book is not legal advice and it's put forth for entertainment purposes. The author and publisher don't take responsibility for the use of any pretext technique discussed nor give you legal advice upon the use of them. We have no liability for your use of pretexts. Laws vary from state to state. Find a competent attorney in your state and rely on his or her advice first.

Acknowledgements

I greatly thank thee;

This book is more than the work of two authors. I gratefully recognize the following individuals and organizations that provided works in this book and other assistance.

Asset Management Service 281-671-4707

www.cellbust.com

"Sharky" the P.I. in New York City

A.A.D.

G.W.G.

B.S.- A major contributor to much misery in my life!

A.J.M.

M.K.V.

G.W.S. – My prayers are with you daily.

E.D.G.

V.A.G. – You're the best!

J.W.D.

L.D.

L.P.

R.L.

All the many repo companies that I have had the pleasure of working with over the past 20 years. To many to name, you know who you are.

If you would like to contribute a pretext to the second edition of this book and have your agency listed, I invite you to contact me via email.
james@hiredgunpub.com

About the Author

James O'Reilly was born and raised in County Cork Ireland. His family moved to America when he was 14 years old. He discovered his fervour for catching bad guys when he watched an undercover officer infiltrate a local gang in his neighborhood, and bring down the entire operation. The excitement of meeting the officer and seeing the busts live sent James on a mission to make the police force. "You can't right every wrong, but you can give it your best."

Now retired, with a beautiful wife and six grown children, James has taken to his Winnebago for some traveling, sight-seeing and relaxation.

Copyright 2013 ©

© James O'Reilly & Hired Gun Publications

www.hiredgunpublications.com

permissions@hiredgunpub.com

All Rights Reserved

"This publication is designed to provide accurate and authoritative information in regard to the subject matter covered. It is sold with the understanding that the publisher is not engaged in rendering legal, accounting, or other professional service. If legal advice or other expert assistance is required, the services of a competent professional person should be sought.

...From the Declaration of Principles jointly adopted by a Committee of the American Bar Association and a Committee of Publishers and Associations."

LIBRARY OF CONGRESS 987654321

ISBN-13: 978-1482392272
ISBN-10: 1482392275

Keyword Index

47657518R00057

Made in the USA
Columbia, SC
03 January 2019